LOVE YOUR JOURNAL

JOURNEY

This journal belongs to

ABOUT YOUR WELLBEING GROWTH JOURNAL

 This journal has been created to help you explore your thoughts, feelings and start to truly believe in yourself as a Remarkable human being.

 In this journal, you'll discover your true potential, sharpen your skills and talents and develop a ton of new ones.

 You will discover that it's OK to make mistakes and get things wrong because these are opportunities to learn valuable lessons (no one ever learnt from getting everything right!).

 This journal will show you that little failures = resilience, confidence and unbelievable growth.

 You'll feel inspired to try new things, take a few risks and step out of your comfort zone.

 You'll learn to embrace and love who you truly are because the world is an incredible place, full of difference and diversity.

 And by the end of it, you will feel super happy and confident and have your feet firmly on the path to reaching your goals.

VISUALISATIONS

In your journal you will find a different visualisation
at the end of each chapter.

These visualisations are designed to change
negative thought patterns by imprinting positive
new ones in your mind.

You can ask someone to read them to you while
you lie down and relax in a quiet space, or read them
first then go on the journey in your mind after.

CONTENTS

Anxiety and Stress

Isn't it so annoying when you hear people say things like:

> **WHAT HAVE YOU GOT TO BE STRESSED ABOUT?**

and

> **YOU DON'T KNOW HOW LUCKY YOU ARE.**

and

> **CHEER UP, YOU HAVE YOUR WHOLE LIFE AHEAD OF YOU.**

You don't know whether to scream at them, break down in tears or run away because actually life for a teenager isn't always fun. It's often confusing and you're not always happy. And although you don't condone violence, you sometimes feel as though you might punch the next person who comes within an inch of you or tries to engage with you in any way.

YOU HAVE PLENTY OF THiNGS TO WORRY ABOUT!

-School or college work pressures and stresses
-Negative thoughts or feelings about yourself
-Anxiety and depression
-Low self-esteem or confidence
-Changes in your body and hormones
-Problems with friends and relationships
-Bullying and threatening behaviours
-Not feeling safe at home or in your town
-Parents separating or divorcing
-Chronic illness or bereavement
-Moving home or changing schools
-Feeling as though you just 'don't fit in'
-Sleep deprivation and low moods
-Phone addictions and bad habits
-Social media pressures and unrealistic goals
-High expectations and pressures from family
-Taking on too much and feeling overwhelmed
-Money and debt problems,

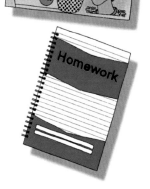

and the list goes on...

Ok so first of all, **STOP and BREATHE.**

No one expects you to cope with all this stuff in one go,
and you don't have to do it all alone.

Anxiety Symptoms

There are plenty of ways our body can react to anxiety, and the physical symptoms can be really grim.

HERE ARE A FEW COMMON SYMPTOMS TO BE AWARE OF:

FEELING RESTLESS OR UNABLE TO SIT STILL

GRINDING TEETH, ESPECIALLY AT NIGHT

NEEDING THE TOILET MORE / LESS OFTEN

PANIC ATTACKS

A CHURNING FEELING IN YOUR STOMACH

WEIGHT LOSS

CONFUSION, UNABLE TO THINK CLEARLY

NAUSEA (FEELING SICK)

PINS AND NEEDLES

SWEATING OR HOT FLUSHES

FAST, SHALLOW BREATHING

LIGHT-HEADED OR DIZZY

HEADACHES

SLEEP LOSS

7

When the horrible symptoms of anxiety are hard to cope with, all we want to do is avoid the situation that stresses us out.

And avoidance does work, but only temporarily.

And sometimes the anxiety can come back worse than before when we allow negative emotions to escalate.

ANXIETY LOOP

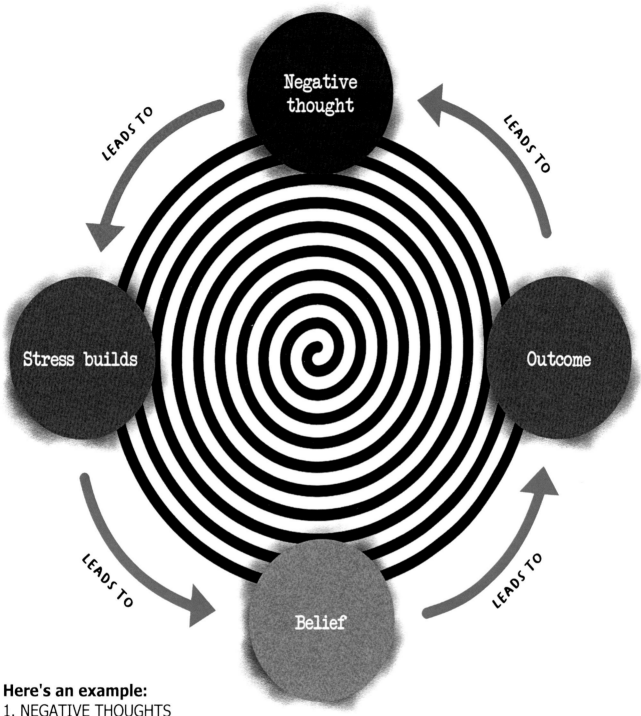

Here's an example:

1. NEGATIVE THOUGHTS
   'I'm not attractive!'
2. STRESS BUILDS
   You start building anxiety symptoms.
3. BELIEF
   'I'll never fit in!'
4. OUTCOME
   Your confidence is affected, you begin to isolate yourself and distance yourself from family and friends.

The longer you allow the loop to continue, the more you start to believe negative and false things about yourself.

What's your Loop?

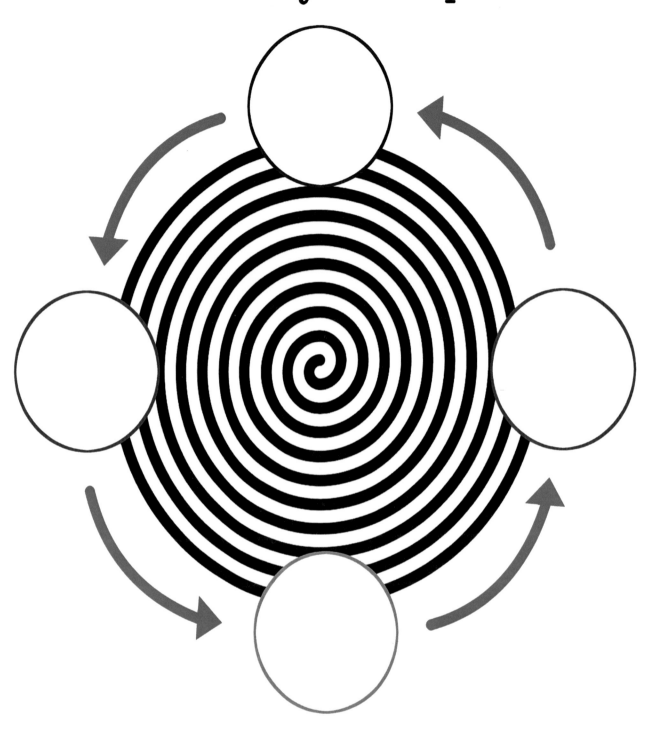

How does your loop affect your outcome?

_____

_____

_____

_____

HOW DO WE BREAK THE CYCLE?

The most effective way of breaking the cycle and overcoming anxiety is by changing the initial thought process.

Sound too simple?

Well, it actually is, but you have to do it on a daily basis to achieve complete success.

For example, change the initial thought... 'I'm not attractive' to, 'I am happy with who I am and how I look'.

You will be suprised at how it can change the course of your loop and the outcome.

(TRY THIS WITH ANY NEGATIVE THOUGHT YOU HAVE THAT CAUSES YOU STRESS!)

Can you **imagine** thinking of a situation that would normally cause you *stress* symptoms and instead feeling really *calm*?

Its actually possible to take control of those difficult feelings by doing this simply excercise regularly.

TO

WE'RE GOING TO FAIL THE TEST THEN OUR FRIENDS WILL THINK WE'RE STUPID THEN THEY'LL STOP TALKING TO US!

WE ARE DOING THE BEST WE CAN, THIS TEST DOES NOT REFLECT MY WORTH AS A PERSON.

TRY NOT TO HANG ONTO YOUR INITIAL NEGATIVE THOUGHT, IT IS NOT TRUE AND DOES NOT REPRESENT WHO YOU ARE AS A PERSON.

Changing the initial thought and producing a new, positive and constructive one will affect the whole cycle and the outcome.

NEW THOUGHT	NEW FEELINGS	NEW ACTIONS	NEW OUTCOMES

Anxiety can sometimes
feel as though you're drowning
in isolation.

But often we can only grow and
recover when we reach out to others to
help keep us afloat. Never feel ashamed
to talk about how you are doing.

POWER ANIMAL VISUALISATION
THE GIFT OF STRENGTH

YOU ARE ABOUT TO GO ON A JOURNEY TO FIND THE HELP YOU NEED, AND THIS HELP WILL COME FROM YOUR VERY OWN *POWER ANIMAL.*

This animal lives on a distant island which is magical and exists only in your mind.

When you arrive on the island you will need to call out to your power animal so they can track and find you. You will say in your mind, *"I AM HERE POWER ANIMAL, I AM HERE, HEAR MY VOICE, I AM HERE".*

Imagine yourself standing by the edge of an ocean, and in the distance, you can see a beautiful island with white sand and a dense green forest behind it. You can fly to this island through the power of your imagination.

See yourself stretching out your arms and slowly rising up off the ground, then when you are ready you fly at speed across the sky to your magical island.

When you arrive on your island you find a comfortable spot, take in the view, and allow your senses to take over. You notice the trees and how they move in the wind, then smell of the wild forest, the crystal clear water gently washing up on the shore and the warm sun on your face.

When you are ready, you call out to your power animal to come and find you and when they do, it will offer you a gift of unimaginable strength that you need in the most challenging times.

You call out to your power animal and wait, and soon you begin to hear rustling in the bushes nearby and slowly you see a magnificent beast step from beyond the trees. It slowly walks towards you then calmly sits at your feet.
You instantly know this animal is loyal to you and you only.

They are powerful in strength and beautiful beyond words and offers you the special gift of bravery and strength.

Picture this beast in your mind now.

How big is he?

Does he have fur or feathers?

What colour is he?

What are his eyes like?

Does he have big claws or teeth?

As you gaze into his eyes, you feel his power soak into every skin cell, every vein and muscle in your body until it becomes you.

You immediately feel fearless of any new challenges that lay ahead and this new strength gives you a massive boost of confidence that you can achieve all that you set out to do in your life.

You thank your power animal for gifting you this strength and you know that he will come again when called in the future.

All you'll need to do is fly to your island and call out to your power animal and he will be there with you.

SIT FOR A MOMENT AFTER YOU HAVE READ THIS VISUALISATION AND USE THE POWER OF YOUR IMAGINATION TO IMAGINE YOUR SPECIAL ISLAND, YOUR MAGNIFICENT POWER ANIMAL, AND THE AMAZING GIFT HE HAS GIVEN YOU.

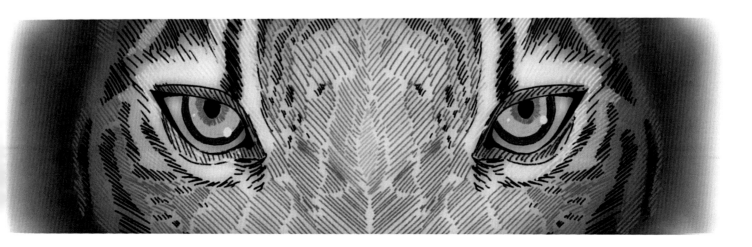

Describe your journey; What did you experience on your way?

_____

_____

_____

_____

What did your power animal look like?

_____

_____

_____

_____

How did you feel after he gifted you the special strength?

_____

_____

_____

_____

Can you think of a time when your power animal could be valuable and why?

_____

_____

_____

_____

CHAPTER 2

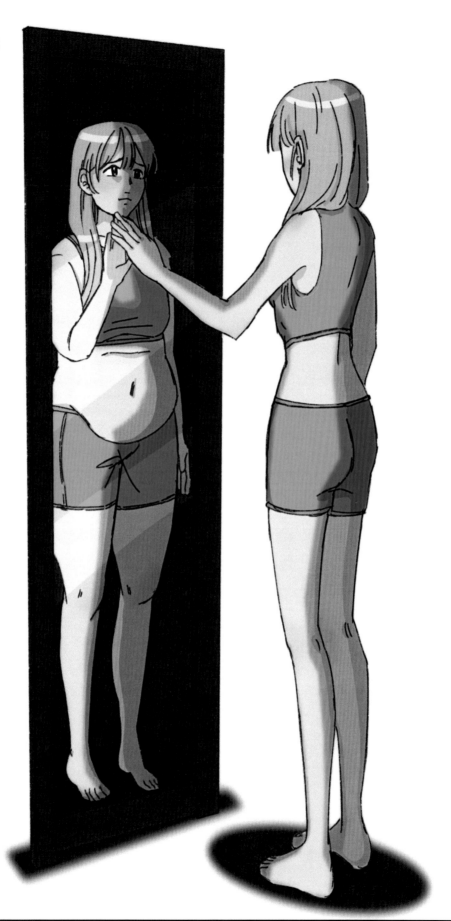

BODY IMAGE and
Acceptance

Vanity vs **BDD**
(What's fake vs What's real)

What is Body Dysmorphia Disorder? – (BDD)

Feeling anxious about the way you look is normal. Wishing you could change a particular feature, stressing about spots, or comparing yourself to an A lister or the popular kid in class are all fairly typical. But body dysmorphic disorder is much more extreme. The words people use to describe themselves are disturbing: I'm hideous. I'm disgusting. I'm revolting and so on.

Dysmorphic means malformed or misshapen, and people struggling with BDD are obsessed with what they believe to be a disfiguring physical flaw. This flaw might be either imagined or a minor flaw that is blown out of proportion.

Some people might believe it to be vanity, but BDD often starts during adolescence, when anxiety is particularly high and can be closely related to OCD, (obsessive compulsive disorder) which can affect both boys and girls equally.

WHAT DO i REALLY LOOK LiKE?

Many people with BDD attempt to have plastic surgery to correct their flaws.

However, these surgeries can actually increase anxiety, and may lead to more expensive, intrusive surgeries which can often spiral out of control and lead to debt and depression.

BDD symptoms to look out for:

- STRESSING ABOUT ONE OR SEVERAL FLAWS

- WORRYING ABOUT MUSCLE SIZE, WEIGHT, COMPLEXION, SCARS OR HAIR

- SPENDING SEVERAL HOURS A DAY IN FRONT OF THE MIRROR

- DIFFICULTY CONCENTRATING IN SCHOOL OR COLLEGE

- RESEARCHING PLASTIC SURGERY OR OTHER CORRECTIVE TREATMENTS

- BECOMING MORE ISOLATED FROM FRIENDS AND FAMILY

- OBSESSING OVER THE PERFECT "SELFIE" AND SOCIAL MEDIA PICTURES

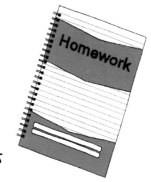

- REPETITIVE BEHAVIOURS SUCH AS REPEATEDLY CHECKING THE MIRROR, PICKING AT SKIN, HAIR ALTERNATIONS AND MAKEUP APPLICATIONS

- THE NEED FOR REASSURANCE OVER PERCEIVED FLAWS

- KEEPING CONCERNS AND ANXIETY A SECRET

- CONTINUOUSLY COMPARING YOUR APPEARANCE TO OTHERS IN MAGAZINES OR SOCIAL MEDIA

- BELIEVING THE FLAWS ARE REAL

Get real!

YOUNG PEOPLE WITH BDD OFTEN FEEL THEY CAN'T BE HAPPY AND ACCEPTED BECAUSE, ALTHOUGH THEY MAY HAVE ACHIEVED STRAIGHT A'S OR PRESENT AMAZING TALENTS, THEY DON'T THINK THEY HAVE THE BODIES THEY'RE 'SUPPOSED TO' HAVE.
UNFORTUNATELY, THIS IS AN UNREALISTIC PERCEPTION OF WHAT'S 'NORMAL' AND IS UNACHIEVABLE BY 90% OF PEOPLE IN SOCIETY.

Fake photoshop - So Don't be fooled!!

SO BE HONEST, HOW MANY TIMES HAVE YOU SEEN A PICTURE ON SOCIAL MEDIA OR IN A MAGAZINE AND THOUGHT, 'I WISH I LOOKED LIKE THAT'? NEWS FLASH: MOST OF THOSE BEAUTIFUL PEOPLE WE SEE WITH FLAWLESS SKIN AND PERFECT BODIES ARE LIES, FAKE AND TOTALLY RIDICULOUS COVER UPS. SO DON'T WASTE YOUR TIME DREAMING OF LOOKING LIKE SOMETHING THAT DOESN'T EXIST.

IT'S OK NOT TO FULLY ACCEPT PARTS OURSELVES THAT WE DON'T LIKE, BUT IT'S WISE TO BE REALISTIC ABOUT WHAT'S 'NORMAL' AND WHAT'S 'FAKE'.

Technology today is a growing market of false representations and coverups. You'll be amazed with the growing amount of computer software that alters a picture dramatically with one click of a button.

- Spots can magically disappear

- You can lose tens of pounds in weight

- Drop 2 dress sizes

- Develop breasts you didn't have or muscles you can only dream of

- Gain inches in height and the list goes on....

Move that body

> EXERCISE IS A GREAT MOOD BOOSTER AND BRILLIANT FOR LOWERING STRESS AND ANXIETY LEVELS. IT'S OK IF YOU'RE NOT NATURALLY ATHLETIC OR REALLY INTO SPORTS AND YOU DON'T HAVE TO BE SUPER FIT TO LOOK AND FEEL GREAT.

Try not to think of exercise as a task you have to do to look good, or you'll risk falling into that void of 'BORING' every time you pick up your gym card!

You could...

- Join a dance group or start your own

- Experiment and try different sports and activities

- Volunteer at a local animal shelter or riding school

- Get a weekend job that involves being active

- Find something that feels right for you!

So forget the gym and get fit doing things that are more fun and inspiring!

GET THE BALL ROLLING *and make a plan that works for you*

Do some research and find some activities that you like the sound of.
Maybe they've been on your list of 'to do's' for a while but you haven't
done anything about it yet.
Or maybe you just want to see what's out there to get inspired!

USE THE TABLE BELOW TO HELP YOU GET MOTIVATED AND MAKE A PLAN

ACTIVITIES AND CLUBS	CONTACT DETAILS	CONTACT MADE AND COMMENTS	START DATES

NEGATIVE BODY CHAT

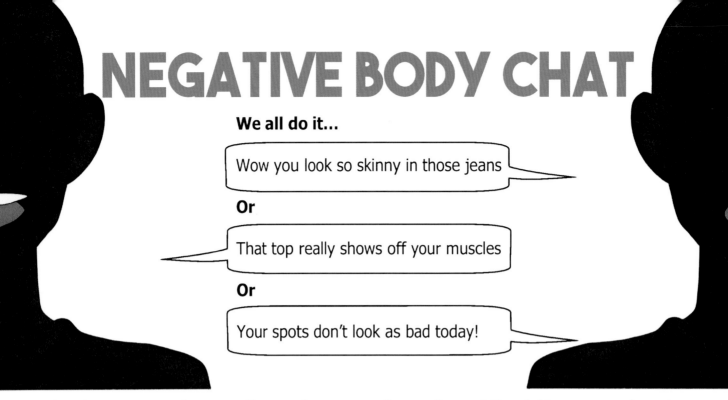

We all do it...

Wow you look so skinny in those jeans

Or

That top really shows off your muscles

Or

Your spots don't look as bad today!

Are those comments supportive, and are we really sending out the right messages by using language like this?

Or do these innocent chats add to the increase pressures of looking a certain way?

And can they actually make us feel worse than we already did?

Is my skin that bad?

Do I need to lose more weight?

Do I look fat in normal clothes?

Do I look gross?

BELIEVE IT OR NOT, THESE KINDS OF CONVERSATIONS (ALTHOUGH WITH THE BEST OF INTENTIONS SOMETIMES) CAN ACTUALLY BE QUITE HARMFUL TO OUR MENTAL HEALTH AND WELLBEING.

How do you think these comments could make young people feel about their appearance?

_____

_____

_____

_____

Can you remember a time when you were asked a similar question? How did you feel?

_____

_____

_____

How do you think this conversation might affect a person's self-esteem in the long run?

_____

_____

_____

_____

MAYBE THERE'S A DIFFERENT WAY WE COULD ASK THOSE SORTS OF QUESTIONS, WITHOUT MAKING A PERSON FEEL EMBARRASSED OR INSECURE

Talking about body parts or skin conditions that are of concern to someone is unhelpful because

_____

_____

_____

BE PROACTIVE AND A LEADER IN POSITIVE BODY CHAT

THINGS YOU COULD DO:

1. Pay attention in group chats and try and put a stop to unhealthy body chats.

2. Make it fun by asking your friends to put money into a jar every time they use negative body chat in a conversation.

3. Be more supportive to friends that you know are feeling insecure about their bodies.

4. Try and cut down on social media time and encourage your friends to do the same.

Can you think of other ways you can encourage healthy body chat?

_____

_____

_____

_____

_____

Learn to love yourself just as you are!

You are more than your body and how people perceive you!

HEART TREASURE VISUALISATION
The Gift of Love

IMAGINE A PRETTY COUNTRY FOOTPATH IN FRONT OF YOU THAT WINDS DOWN TOWARDS A BEAUTIFUL SANDY BEACH. YOU CAN HEAR THE WATER AT THE BOTTOM, LAZILY LAPPING UP ONTO THE SHORE AND YOU CAN FEEL THE WARM SUN ON YOUR FACE AS YOU WALK.

This is your special place and nobody else knows about it or goes there. See it clearly in your mind. Hear the sounds that are present and the smells around you in the fresh sea breeze. Each breath you take you are aware of how completely relaxed you feel and how much you are looking forward to taking off your shoes and dipping your toes in the water.

As you reach the end of the pathway you look out to sea and notice a small wooden box sticking out of the sand, and the hinges are a shiny metal and glimmering in the sunlight. You walk towards it and see a key lying on the sand beside the box, so you decide to try the lock and look inside.
As soon as the box lid starts to open you can see a bright light bursting out of it and then you notice a beautiful glowing, heart-shaped jewel lying on a soft velvet blanket within the chest and it has your name on it.

HEART TREASURE VISUALISATION
The Gift of Love

You decide to touch it and immediately as it touches your skin it projects feelings of love, confidence, and self-worth.

You pick up the treasure and hold it in front of your heart and feel the love radiate from it and straight into you and it feels amazing. Any fears, insecurities or worries you had before have now completely disappeared as you hold this treasure close to your heart. You stand there for a while, radiating these wonderful feelings of love, then when you feel you have had enough you gently place it back in the box and keep the key with you to use another time.

As you slowly walk barefoot along the beach you feel calm and safe, and you know you can come back to this place whenever you want to hold your heart jewel again and be reminded of how truly wonderful you are.

How do you feel when you hold your treasure?

_____

_____

_____

Can you remember a time when you felt strong, happy, and secure in yourself?

_____

_____

_____

Describe or draw what your treasure looks or feels like below:

CHAPTER 3

DIFFERENCE

IS GOOD AND MAKES US WHO WE ARE AND THE WORLD A WONDERFUL PLACE

EQUALITY AND DIVERSITY, OR MULTICULTURALISM, IS ABOUT PROMOTING, ACCEPTING, AND RESPECTING THE DIFFERENCES BETWEEN US ALL. IT MEANS TO BE FAIR AND TREAT PEOPLE AS EQUALS, REGARDLESS OF THEIR RACE, GENDER, AGE, DISABILITY, RELIGION, OR SEXUAL ORIENTATION.

TRANSGENDER
& Gender Dysmorphia

KNOW THE FACTS

Being transgender means that a person's gender at birth, (boy or girl) does not match the gender they feel within themselves.

Young people who are transgender feel very strongly that they are not the gender assigned to them at birth. It might feel as though you were a boy trapped in a girl's body, or a girl trapped in a boy's body which would be very confusing and upsetting.
Being transgender could also make a young person feel extremely uncomfortable about their bodies as they grow and develop in the puberty stages and make it extremely challenging to accept the body they have been given.

Sometimes, the difference between how a transgender person was born and how they feel inside causes extreme distress which is called gender dysphoria. Although these difficult emotions can be very unsettling for a young person it is not a mental health disorder, and not all transgender people experience gender dysphoria. Gender dysphoria is only diagnosed when a person is struggling emotionally with their gender on a daily basis, and they may need extra support to help them cope with their emotions.

KNOWLEDGE iS POWER! 💪

Learn more about trans and gender diverse people. Do some internet searches and check out articles, books, blogs, music, shows and video games about their experiences.

_____

_____

_____

_____

SEXUAL iDENTiTY VS GENDER iDENTiTY!

Are these things the same? Do some research and write your answers below.

_____

_____

_____

_____

DO YOU KNOW ANYONE WHO MiGHT BE EXPERiENCiNG GENDER iDENTiTY iSSUES? 🖤

If yes, think of ways you might help and support them and write them below.

_____

_____

_____

_____

PUBERTY

Why am I so emotional?

Ok, so you already know about the obvious changes during puberty:

Girls, you have hair growing from places you didn't think hair grew!

Your breasts are growing at different paces which is freaking you out and they are so painful with the slightest of touch.

You're noticing white discharge stains on your knickers and your spots and tummy cramps are off the scale.

Your hips are changing shape and you are developing a full sized adult bottom.

Boys, your vocal cords are making some mighty strange noises and can't seem to settle between a middle or low octave.

And you keep having bizarre dreams but are too embarrassed to tell your parents.

You have three hairs growing from your chin and no amount of shaving increases that number.

THESE CHANGES CAN ALL BE EMBARRASSING AND UPSETTING, BUT WHAT ABOUT THE UNSEEN THINGS?

THE RADICAL CHANGES HAPPENING IN YOUR HEAD AT THIS TIME MIGHT EXPLAIN WHY YOU FEEL LIKE CRYING FOR NO REASON ONE MINUTE AND FLYING INTO A RAGE THE NEXT.

Inside your brain – *Here's the science bit*

Adolescence is a time of major growth and development inside the teenage brain.
The brain develops really quickly in the first 3 to 5 years of life, and most things are in place by the age of 9.

The last part to develop is the front part of the brain, called the prefrontal cortex. This is the part that helps us with decision making and planning, problem solving and controlling reactions. Because the prefrontal cortex is still developing in adolescence, teenagers have no choice but to rely on a different part of the brain called the amygdala to make decisions and solve problems.

Unfortunately, the amygdala part of the brain is linked with emotions, impulses like the 'fight or flight reaction', anger and unpredictable behaviour.

So next time someone older or younger gets frustrated with you, or you react in a way that's out of character, you are perfectly within your right to blame it on your undeveloped prefrontal cortex.

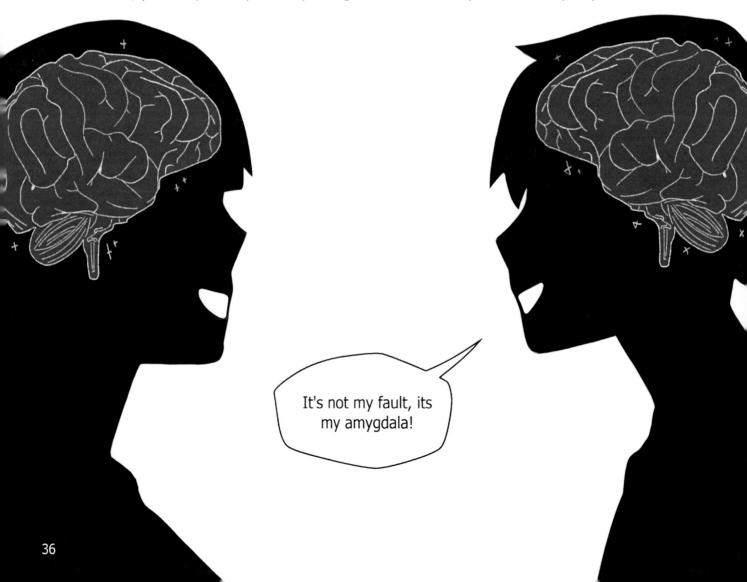

It's not my fault, its my amygdala!

CAN YOU THINK OF A TIME WHEN YOU FELT OUT OF CONTROL OR WERE SUPRISED BY YOUR OWN REACTIONS TO SOMETHING?

What happened?

_____

_____

_____

_____

How did you feel?

_____

_____

_____

_____

What calmed you down?

_____

_____

_____

_____

What else could you do to help calm down and avoid more stress?

_____

_____

_____

_____

MAKE A POSTER TO CELEBRATE A *CULTURE!*

You could make the poster about food, fashion, the many languages throughout that culture or about different religions and traditions within it.

HAPPY
AFRICA

INDEPENDENCE,
FREEDOM, AND AFRICAN PRIDE

Write a couple of interesting facts about your chosen culture!

Fact 1 _____

_____

_____

Fact 2 _____

_____

_____

MY FAMILY, MY CULTURE AND ME

Who is in your family?

_____

What is your cultural background or religion?

_____

Do you celebrate any religious festivals and what does that involve?

_____

How different is your family compared to your friends?

_____

What do you enjoy most about your family?

_____

What would you change and why?

_____

What makes you proud of your family, culture, or religion?

_____

WHY NOT CELEBRATE A DiFFERENT CULTURE EACH WEEK BY TRYiNG DiFFERENT FOODS, LiSTENiNG TO THEiR TRADiTiONAL MUSiC, PLAYiNG GAMES, LEARNiNG FACTS, WATCHiNG ViDEOS?

Design a menu

Design a menu and host a meal for your friends for a cultural celebration of your choice such as Chinese New Year, Diwali, Easter or Ramadan to raise awareness of different cultures and religions.

Why did you choose this celebration?

_____

What new things did you learn about this culture?

_____

What dish did you and your friends enjoy the most?

_____

STARTER

MAIN

DESSERT

CULTURE & DIVERSITY QUIZ

PLAY THiS WiTH A GROUP OF FRiENDS, FAMiLY OR ASK
YOUR TEACHER TO PLAY iT iN CLASS WiTH THE OTHER STUDENTS.

(Get into two teams – The team with most answers correct is the winner)

1. **Which CONTINENT is the most linguistically diverse in the world?**

2. **If you dislike someone you don't even know, simply because that person has a certain religion, this would be called what?**

3. **It's always obvious if someone has a disability.**
True or False

4. **Which country is known as "the land of no rivers"?**

5. **Which country has been labelled the most diverse?**

6. **The words handicapped or wheelchair bound are politically correct words to use.**
True or False?

7. **Being transgender is the same as being gay or bisexual.**
True or False?

8. **Gay couples cannot legally be married in the UK. True or false?**

9. **What year were women over 18 years of age legally entitled to vote?**

   1818
   1918
   2018

10. **In China it was illegal to have more than one child.**
True or False?

CULTURE & DIVERSITY QUIZ

PLAY THiS WiTH A GROUP OF FRiENDS, FAMiLY OR ASK
YOUR TEACHER TO PLAY iT iN CLASS WiTH THE OTHER STUDENTS.

ANSWERS

1. Answer - **Africa! The continent is home to anywhere from 800 to 1,500 of the world's languages.**

2. Answer – **Prejudice**

3. Answer – **False**

4. Answer - **Saudi Arabia. Most of their fresh water comes from desalinization plants or underground reservoirs.**

5. Answer - **In almost every category—culturally, economically, climatically, racially, linguistically, ethnically, and religiously, India is either the most diverse country in the world or the runner-up.**

6. Answer – **False**

7. Answer – **False**

8. Answer – **False**

9. Answer – **1918**

10. Answer – **True (The policy was changed due to the aging population).**

Hot Air Balloon Visualisation
The gift of Acceptance

Imagine walking up a long, steep hill and when you reach the top you are amazed to see lots of brightly coloured hot air balloons sitting on the ground below. As you stand there in wonder for a few moments, you notice that each one has different colours and patterns on it. You watch in astonishment as each one gently lifts off the ground and dreamily floats up into the air without effort before drifting lazily across the fields and towns below.

These balloons look like an incredible display of colour and patterns in the sky; one has crashing waves over a sunset and one has a night sky with star formations and the milky way; One ballon has an incredible rainbow over a bustling city; while another has the picture of a beautiful snowy mountain in front of a bright sun. You observe how wonderful it is to be witness to so much diversity through the vivid colour and splendour of hot air balloons; where people from all over the world have come together to enjoy and share their true passion in life by displaying rich landscapes from their country's origins and celebrating the differences they all bring to the planet.

You suddenly feel inspired to step out of your comfort zone and try something incredible and different, so you choose your favourite balloon and walk towards it. You see a man standing inside the basket section of the balloon and he says with a huge smile on his face that he 'has been waiting for you to find the courage to step inside'. You know instantly that you will be safe in this balloon and you see that all your favourite snacks and drinks sit nicely packed into the corner of the basket as you gently lift off the ground.

Hot Air Balloon Visualisation
The gift of Acceptance

The sky is blue, the sun is shining and as the balloon starts to move off the ground you notice how calm you feel inside and you can't wait to get higher in the sky. You watch as the houses and trees get smaller and smaller, like little pieces of Lego. The higher you get in the sky, the happier and more confident you feel inside and accepting of who you are on this journey of life. You realise that the differences we all share make up the wonderful diversity of our planet and give us valuable lessons to grow and flourish in our lives.

You make the decision at that moment to fully accept and embrace who you are in life and within everything you set out to do. You feel inspired to try other adventures in the future because you know how much more confident and resilient you will feel as a result. As you stand there gazing out across the sky at all the other different balloons, you start to feel really strong inside. All the challenges you've faced and overcome, all the lessons you've learnt, are helping you to become truly remarkable.

After a while you give the signal to the man that you'd like to go back down to the ground and you realise that this balloon ride will be here for you whenever you want it in the future. Any time you feel you might need a boost of confidence or reassurance that you are doing just great, you can walk to your amazing balloon and set off on another adventure in the sky.

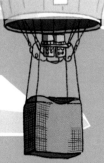

What did your balloon like and why did you select that one?

_____

_____

_____

Describe your journey. What did you see on your way?

_____

_____

_____

How did it make you feel when you were up there?

_____

_____

_____

Draw a picture of your balloon here:

CHAPTER 4

MANAGING ANGER

WE ALL GET ANGRY

In small doses, anger is an appropriate, normal, and a healthy emotion. It helps us to express our feelings, stand up for what is right and protect ourselves and our loved ones.

But when anger escalates or becomes frequent it can become a problem and bring unfortunate and unwanted consequences.

We're like a pressure cooker starting to boil when something triggers our anger!

EXPLOSIVE

ANGRY

FRUSTRATED

MILDLY
IRRITATED

1 TRIGGER

What kind of things can trigger an anger reaction with you?

2 EMOTION

How do those things make you feel inside?

3 REACTION

How would you normally react?

ANGER PATH

In the boxes below, describe one of your triggers, the emotion you might feel and a common reaction.
Then in the last box, write or draw a more ideal reaction.

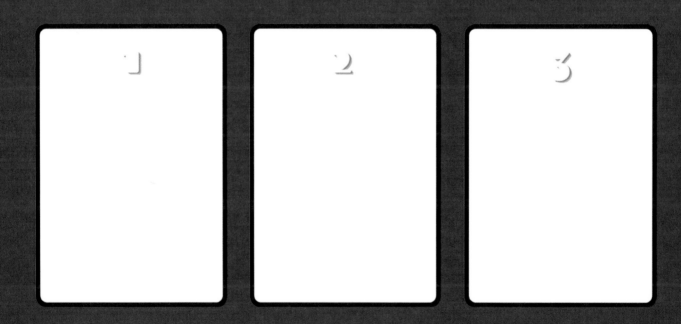

1

2

3

How would you prefer to react to those triggers?

DRAW A PiCTURE OF WHAT YOUR ANGER LOOKS LiKE TO YOU

Imagine your anger as a person or some kind of beast you can communicate with.

What would you say to it?

_____

_____

What name would you give it?

_____

_____

How would you reason with it or help it to calm down?

_____

_____

WHAT YOU CONTROL AND WHAT YOU DON'T

The majority of reasons we get stressed are because of other people. But we have no control over their lives, what they say or what they do.

THINGS OUTSIDE OF MY CONTROL

Other people's actions

Other people's words

Other people's life choices

Other people's feelings

Other people's mistakes

Other people's consequences

Other people's plans

THINGS I AM IN CONTROL OF

My words

My actions

My feelings

My choices

My values

My future plans and goals

My life

You are the boss of your life. Don't let others take any of those things away from you by causing you unnecessary stress which may result in bad decisions and failed attempts at your life decisions and goals.

Anger can be a tough emotion to control. Normally we may try to bottle our emotions inside, so we don't upset those around us.

The best way to prevent our emotions getting out of control is to find ways to manage stress and find constructive and healthy coping mechanisms.

TOP TIPS FOR DEALING WITH
ANGER AND FRUSTRATION

REMEMBER

YOU CAN ONLY CONTROL YOUR OWN THOUGHTS AND ACTIONS, NOT OTHER PEOPLE'S.

THINK

WHERE AM I ON THE STRESS METRE RIGHT NOW?

ASK YOURSELF

IF I LOSE CONTROL RIGHT NOW, AM I GOING TO ACHIEVE WHAT I WANT FOR MY LIFE NOW OR IN THE FUTURE?

PRACTISE

TECHNIQUES THAT HELP YOU CALM DOWN SUCH AS BREATHING SLOWLY, LISTENING TO MUSIC, CHATTING TO A FRIEND , DOING SOMETHING CREATIVE OR GOING FOR A RUN.

DON'T

BE A TICKING TIME BOMB OR REACT BEFORE YOU HAVE THOUGHT ABOUT THE CONSEQUENCES.

IF ALL ELSE FAILS

AND YOU KNOW YOU ARE GOING TO LOSE IT, WALK AWAY BEFORE YOU REGRET YOUR ACTIONS.

CREATING CALM

FOCUS ON COLOURING IN THIS MANDALA
AND LET YOUR CREATIVITY FLOW!

CALMING CARDS!

Here are some cards you can cut out for when you need help finding coping methods

 Talk to Friends

Create or Colour!

Take Deep Breaths

Eat some Good Food

 Listen to Music

Watch a Movie or Show

Think Happy Thoughts

Pet an Animal

WOULD YOU RATHER...?

(Tick the box you agree with)

A Be controlling over others
B Have control over your own emotions and actions

A Push in a queue because it's too long
B Wait your turn or join it another day

A Be heard in every conversation with all people
B Be happy to step back occasionally and let others talk

A Be a loud rock star
B Work in an animal rescue centre

A Live in a mansion in a noisy city
B Live in a cottage in the country

A Own a big fierce dog
B Own a calm cuddly kitten

A Fight your way through a crowd to get out
B Walk the longer way around the crowd to get out

A Take on a dare from your friends, even if it risks your safety
B Think twice about the consequences and refuse to do it

A Put pressure on someone to do something for you
B Ask, but accept their answer if it's a no

A Have those trainers now and get upset if you don't
B Be willing to save up and get them later

A Scream to get your point across in an argument
B Discuss your point calmly and listen to other points of view also

A Punch, kick and use aggression when you're angry
B Take some deep breaths and go for a walk to calm down

A Lose friends and be right
B Keep friends and agree to disagree

A Leave your little brother at home so he doesn't cramp your style
B Take your little brother to the park where your friends will be

A Kick-off in class in front of other students and risk being suspended
B Take control of your emotions and not get in trouble

RESULTS

Count up how many A' and B's you have.

If you have mainly A's:

You are on a learning path of self-discovery. You are strong willed but occasionally lack control and make unhealthy decisions. Work on finding your inner strength and confidence and the rest will come naturally in time.

If you have mainly B's:

You have control of your emotions and great empathy for others. Your intuition is strong, and you make healthy decisions. Keep doing what you're doing, and you will succeed in many areas of your life.

MAGICAL BUBBLE VISUALISATION

IMAGINE YOU ARE WALKING IN THE COUNTRYSIDE ON A SUNNY DAY AND SUDDENLY, IN THE DISTANCE YOU NOTICE BRIGHT SPARKLY BUBBLES SLOWLY BOUNCING ACROSS A GRASSY FIELD.

Some are small, and some are as big as you,

gently bouncing off each other as they glide along.

You walk towards them, and as you get closer you reach out to

touch one of the biggest bubbles and you notice how soft it feels as you

push your hand against it. You reach inside the bubble, and it doesn't burst,

so you take off your shoes and slowly step inside.

You gently drift around, swishing and rocking forward and backward across the

green grass and you realise how calm and safe you feel inside this bubble, like

it has an invisible protective force field around the outside.

A force field that stops any outside influences from coming into contact

with you. A force field that helps you to stay in control of your

feelings and reactions. A force field that strengthens you and

builds your confidence so that you are reassured once

more of how truly remarkable you are.

MAGICAL BUBBLE VISUALISATION

You gently glide up in the air in your protective

bubble and look down on all the other bubbles calmly bouncing

around over the swishing green grass. Then when it is

time, and you feel you would like to be on the ground once more,

you gently lean forward, and the bubble begins to move slowly to the

ground again before coming to a final stop.

You loved being in your protective bubble and realise that anytime you feel you

need to take control of your emotions or reactions and stay away from

outside influences that are challenging to you, you can simply imagine

the safety of your protective bubble and step inside to enjoy

all the wonderful and supportive feelings it gives you.

How did it feel to be inside your magical bubble?

_____

_____

_____

_____

Can you remember a time in the past when this bubble would have been helpful?

_____

_____

_____

_____

When might you use this bubble visualisation in the future?

CHAPTER 5

_____

_____

_____

_____

Pros and Cons of Social Media

Ok, so it's obvious that social media has it's really good advantages in society today. As technology is advancing and we are becoming more reliant on it's benefits for training, employment and social interactions. We have to stay on top of the ever-changing market.

But it's also true that social media can be overwhelming and unhealthy if we don't get the balance right.

HERE'S A FEW PROS & CONS TO CONSIDER...

PROS

- Great opportunities for further education

- It can be a good way to learn new skills (for free)

- Social media can help teach about money and budgeting

- It can sometimes enhance creativity and inspire us to create more

- Can help with employment opportunities and work experience

CONS

- It can be highly addictive

- Young people can often think it defines them

- Often it can bring unwanted attention from predators or revenge seekers

- Social media can be too focused on appearance and cause insecurities

- Is often the cause of cyber bullying or trolling

CAN YOU THINK OF ANY MORE PROS AND CONS?

PRO:_____

CON:_____

PRO:_____

CON:_____

How has social media helped you personally?

_____

_____

_____

_____

What has put you off social media or caused problems for you?

_____

_____

_____

_____

REMEMBER, iF ANYONE MAKES YOU FEEL UNCOMFORTABLE ONLiNE DON'T iGNORE iT.

TELL SOMEONE YOU TRUST BEFORE THiNGS ESCALATE.

AND NEVER TELL ANY STRANGERS ONLiNE WHERE YOU LiVE OR ANY OTHER PERSONAL iNFORMATiON.

CYBERBULLYING

'Cyberbulling' is the use of digital technologies with an intent to offend, humilate, threaten, harass or abuse someone!

TROLLS ARE PEOPLE WHO DELIBERATELY LEAVE OFFENSIVE COMMENTS ON THE INTERNET TO CAUSE A BIG DRAMA AND GET ATTENTION SO THEY CAN GET MORE VIEWS OR FOLLOWERS

DID YOU KNOW?

CYBER BULLYING IS ILLEGAL, AND YOU CAN GO TO PRISON FOR TROLLING SOMEONE

What is Cyberbullying?

CYBERBULLYING IS BULLYING ONLINE AND OVER ANY FORM OF SOCIAL MEDIA PLATFORM WHICH INTENDS TO CAUSE HARM AND DISTRESS TO ANOTHER PERSON.

HERE'S SOME EXAMPLES TO LOOK OUT FOR:

Spreading malicious and abusive rumours and gossiping

Emailing or texting you with threatening or intimidating remarks

Mobbing (a group or gang that target you)

Harassing you repeatedly

Intimidation and blackmail

Stalking you online and continually harassing you

Posting humiliating images or videos without your consent

Posting your private details online without consent

General bullying or stalking

Grooming (encouraging harmful or inappropriate behaviour)

Setting up a false profile, identity fraud or identity theft

Using gaming sites to attack or bully you

Theft, fraud, or deception over the internet

KEEP SAFE AND KEEP ONE STEP AHEAD OF BULLIES

WHAT'S APPROPRIATE & WHAT'S NOT?

CAN YOU SPOT ANYTHING IN THESE POSTS THAT MIGHT BE SEEN
AS INAPPROPRIATE OR RISKY?

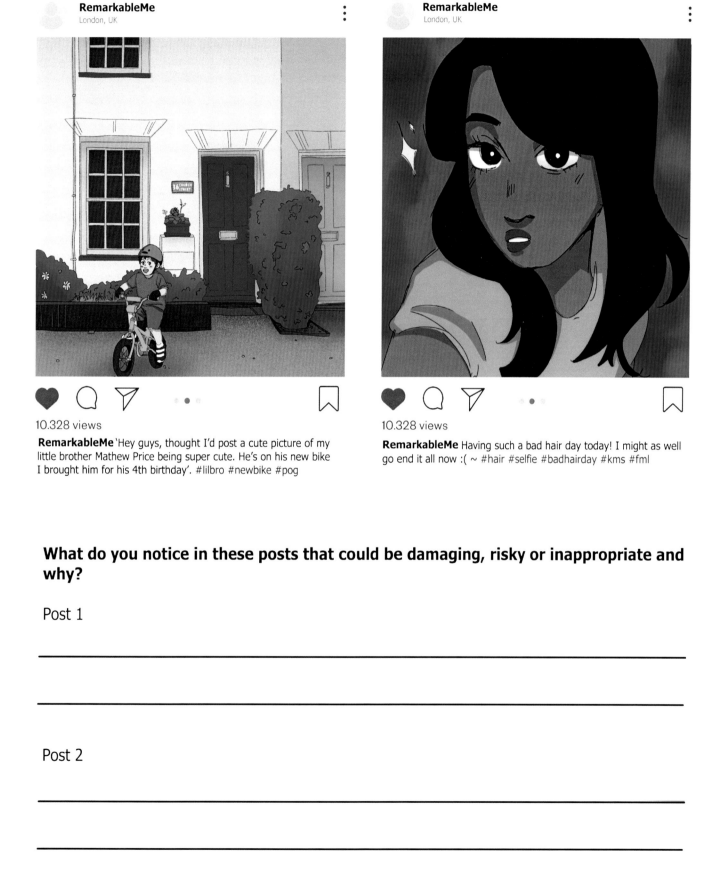

What do you notice in these posts that could be damaging, risky or inappropriate and why?

Post 1

_____

_____

Post 2

_____

_____

Social media can be a brilliant hub for creativity and a great way of keeping in touch with other people and current events from all over the globe.

But it's also important to recognise the potential threats and dangers that can come with being in such an open space.

(DESIGN YOUR POST HERE)

Create your own App

What's your App called?

_____

_____

What does it do?

_____

_____

Who will use your App? i.e what are their interests and age groups?

_____

_____

How will you make it safe and healthy for people to use?

_____

_____

Design your App below (keep your idea simple and memorable):

Tree House Visualisation

You start your journey by walking down a twisted cobbled pathway which leads into a beautiful ancient wood at the bottom. As you enter the woods and press your way through the trees you see beams of light shooting down from the top of the leaves onto the ground ahead of you and it looks so beautiful.

The woods are filled with wildflowers and butterflies and you're feeling really happy and relaxed with not a care in the world. Any worries or sadness you have been feeling are now starting to fall off you like leaves falling from a tree.

As you continue to walk you begin to hear voices in the distance: Happy voices, laughing and singing and having fun, so you decide to investigate. As the voices get louder you notice that they are coming from above you, so you look up into the trees and to your amazement, you notice the most incredible tree house.

It's a large tree house with a long yellow ladder and it sounds like there's a party or some kind of celebration going on inside it. As you listen more closely, you realise the voices inside are familiar to you. They are voices of people that you know well and love.

Friends and family you haven't seen in a long time and have been really missing. You are so excited to see them and hug them and catch up properly, so you call up to them and one by one you see their big smiley faces peering out. They call down to you asking you to climb up and as you climb the ladder you can feel your heart filling with love and happiness, and you know that it won't be long before you're all hugging and chatting and sharing news of what you've been up to.

Tree House Visualisation

As you reach the top, they pull you into the tree house. You fall into their arms and you feel so safe and happy. After some time hugging and chatting and laughing together you realise that all those times when you have been feeling lonely or sad had just disappeared.

Those feelings that had been really getting you down had simply faded away in one moment.

In fact, they are so distant to you now that you can't even remember feeling sad in the first place.

You realise that all those messages and posts you have shared on your phone and social media have meant nothing compared with the real times spent together.

You know how important friendship and family is and you want to treasure the moments you share with them all from now on. You remember that your friends and family will always be there for you to share special memories with you because you are loved, and they know that you love them.

Love is stronger and more important than anything. It's stronger than time or distance. It's more powerful than towns and countries and love always finds its way into our hearts and into our lives.

And after a while you decide it's time to leave this place, and you feel reassured that you can come back here at any point in the future. So, you climb down the ladder, then slowly venture back into the woods and up the winding pathway that brought you here.

You feel so happy and content that you had this experience and so grateful for all the special memories you have of those that are closest to you.

What did your house look like?

_____

_____

_____

Who was in your tree house?

_____

_____

_____

How did you feel when you saw your family and friends again?

_____

_____

_____

Did this visualisation remind you of anyone you have missed in your life?

_____

_____

_____

Are there any changes you would like to make to your friend groups or family relationships and why?

_____

_____

_____

CHAPTER 6

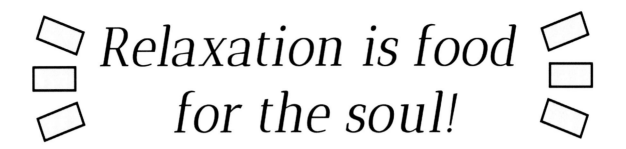

Relaxation is food for the soul!

YOU CAN FLiP TO THiS CHAPTER EVERY TiME YOU NEED iDEAS OR GUiDANCE AROUND CHiLL OUT TECHNiQUES AND RELAXATiON.

There are so many ways to calm your mind and body that we have decided to dedicate a whole chapter to it, and you'll be amazed to discover that there are so many more relaxation skills to discover than simply deep breathing exercises.

Perhaps there are even techniques you have never heard of which is great because in the world of difference and diversity, we can explore all realms of unique ways to not only relax, but be inspired to make positive changes in our lives.

The Power of Meditation

WHAT iS iT?

Meditation not only helps us to relax but it can also reduce anxiety, improve memory, and help us to feel more inspired to be creative and make important changes.

KNOW YOUR BRAiNWAVES

We all have brainwaves, and they are just one feature of our mind that help us to experience everything in life, and the best thing is that ....

You have control over them!

When we meditate, we can tap into our **alpha** and **theta** waves which automatically help us to feel relaxed, calm, and super creative.

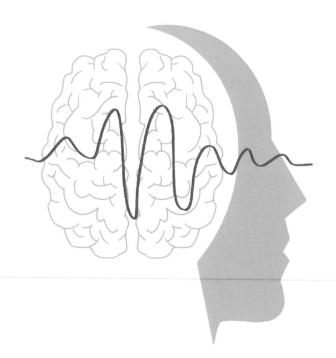

Science Bit

MEET YOUR 5 MAIN TYPES OF BRAIN WAVES

Gamma brainwaves: Helps us with awareness, learning, consciousness, and problem solving and homework.

Beta brainwaves: Work when we are busy thinking and concentrating in conversations or focusing on a task.

Alpha brainwaves: Are present when the mind is calm, relaxed, when we are being creative or just before we fall asleep. (They also increase during meditation).

Theta brainwaves: Are active during deep meditation, daydreaming, or while we carry out boring tasks like emptying a dishwasher or taking a taking a shower.

Delta brainwaves: These are slow brainwaves which occur during deep sleep.

LET'S HAVE A GO AT MEDITATION

1. Make sure you are in a quiet place where you won't be disturbed.

2. Sit or lie down comfortably and close your eyes.

3. Think about your breathing now and gently slow it down, taking 3 deep inhales in through your nose and slow exhales out through your mouth.

4. Try to focus your mind on your breath as you begin to relax your body from the top of your head and down through every part of your body until you reach the bottom of your toes.

5. Try and keep your breath at a slow even pace, not speeding up at all, as our mind sometimes wants to jump ahead. Allow it to remain focused on slow, evenly paced breaths.

You have tapped into your Alpha brain waves when your body and mind is totally relaxed. **WELL DONE!**

There are many different levels of meditation we can achieve.
You may just want to stop here at the relaxed mind and body stage which is perfectly fine.

OR YOU MAY WANT TO GO DEEPER.

When we go deeper, we tap into the **Theta brain waves**, which is when we can actually change our thought process from negative to positive. The more we practice meditation, the more successful we can be at achieving the right results.

THETA STAGE

When you are totally relaxed, image yourself in a safe, calm, and happy place. Perhaps it's a place you have been before, or maybe it's a place that exists only in your mind. Enjoy all the sounds, feelings, and images in this place. Then when you are ready, think of the thing you might want to change in your life.

For example:

If it is something negative such as thinking badly of yourself or getting too angry, you could image a large bin next to you and throwing those negative and unhelpful thoughts and feelings into the bin then closing it tight.

Or perhaps you might want to feel more confident or happy or some other positive aspect of your life. You could then imagine these positive things covering you like soft warm wind or gentle waves rolling over your body as you lie on a sandy beach.

You can be as creative as you like in meditation, as long as it feels right and comfortable to you. When you find what works, try and practice the same process until you notice those positive changes in your life.

The power of our MIND is a truly incredible thing once we know how to actively use our Theta brain waves.

WRITE YOUR EXPERIENCES OF ACHIEVING THE THETA WAVES DURING MEDITATION BELOW:

How did you feel?

_____

_____

_____

_____

What did you see in your special place?

_____

_____

_____

_____

What changes have you noticed since practising meditation?

_____

_____

_____

_____

SPEND TIME IN NATURE

We are actually genetically programmed to find trees, plants, water, and other nature elements.

That is why we automatically feel more relaxed when we're amongst it.

Spending time in natural environments can also be a good distraction from pain and discomfort and it can be healing for our mind and help fight anxiety or depression.

Ideas to Connect with Nature

Grow or pick your own food

Look for local farms or orchards that let you pick fruit to buy. You might also enjoy foraging for wild fruit in the forest. Just make sure you double check you're not picking anything poisonous before putting it in your mouth.

Bring nature inside

Try growing herbs or flowers at home. Or you could take photos of your favourite places in nature and use them as backgrounds on a device or as part of a school or college project. You could even record nature sounds like birdsong, ocean waves or rainfall and listen to them when you feel stressed.

Outdoor activities

Eat more meals outdoors such as picnics in the garden or at a local park. You could even suggest the occasional BBQ with friends or extended family.

Watch the stars and look out for shooting ones or the milky way on a clear night. There are plenty of stargazing websites and apps to help you recognise different stars and it can be really fun to recognise different constellations and planets.

Try exercising outside such as running, cycling, walking a dog or joining a local outdoor sports club. You could do it by yourself or get a bunch of friends to do it with you.

Help the environment

Have you ever thought of volunteering at a local project? How about joining a conservation project to help our environment? Just do a google search for ones in your area and see what pops up.

There is so much you can do such as help plant new trees or plants to help bumblebees.
You could help build an animal habitat such as a safe place for hedgehogs or a fox den, or perhaps build a pond for other wildlife to inhabit.

RECORD YOUR EXPERIENCES OF BEING iN NATURE

Where did you go?

_____

_____

How did it feel when you were there?

_____

_____

What positive changes to your life or the environment have you made?

_____

_____

What other things do you want to explore outside?

_____

_____

Draw a picture of your favourite place in nature:

Connect with Animals!

DOGS AND CATS

Have you ever noticed how stroking a dog or cat can leave you feeling rather relaxed and happy after?

Well, believe it or not, the simple act of petting animals releases the 'happy hormone' in our body called serotonin, and it is this hormone that is responsible for the happy feelings.

The happier we are, the more our stress levels reduce and the less anxiety we feel.

Dogs in particular can be great companions also as they love us no matter what.

They don't judge us if we make a mistake, and they don't criticise us for acting a fool.

They just love us unconditionally which makes for the perfect friendship and stops us feeling lonely.

Try pet-sitting or dog walking to get your serotonin working, or you could offer to be a pet sitter in your local neighbourhood.

What about volunteering to walk dogs for an animal shelter, or asking a friend if you could borrow their dog for an occasional evening or weekend walks?

EAT - EQUINE-ASSISTED THERAPY

This structured time spent with horses to help promote physical, emotional and mental wellbeing. Since the animals have behaviours in common with humans, such as the way they socialise with each other and respond to others, it is easy for people to create a connection with them.

EAT has been known to help with so many different issues such as Anxiety, Autism, Cerebral Palsy, Dementia, Depression, Brain injuries, Behavioural issues, Trauma and many other mental health problems.

Equine Therapy can also help people to build confidence, resilience, communication, trust and social skills.

Make enquiries with a reputable stable or sanctuary and ask if they need volunteers so you can help out and get to know the horses.

You could even enquire at a local Equine centre to see what therapeutic services they are offering.

But very importantly...

Don't start wandering across fields in order to spend valuable time with a horse you don't know, as they are powerful animals and can cause a lot of physical damage if they feel afraid or threatened.

Make sure you contact the owner of an organisation before approaching a horse so you and the animal remain safe.

RECORD YOUR EXPERIENCES

Have you spent time with a dog, cat, horse or any other furry animal recently?

_____

_____

_____

_____

What activity did you do?

_____

_____

_____

_____

How did you feel during and after and how has it benefited you?

_____

_____

_____

_____

Have you contacted any local organisations and enquired about volunteering?

_____

_____

_____

POWER OF DRUMMING

YOU MAY WONDER WHY WE HAVE LISTED DRUMMING OF ALL THINGS IN THE CHILL OUT SECTION OF THIS JOURNAL. WELL, ACTUALLY THE DRUM CAN BE INCREDIBLY THERAPEUTIC AND EXHILARATING ON MANY LEVELS.

There is no other instrument quite like the drum which is considered to be the 'heartbeat' of all music and rhythms around the world.

The drum is the oldest musical instrument in the world and dates back to 5500BC. Learning to play the drums is an incredibly rewarding activity both physical and mentally.

HERE'S SOME MORE BENEFITS:

1. Drumming encourages relaxation

The communication between the brain and the body whilst drumming allows us to tap into our Theta brain waves if the tempo is consistent and at the same volume, releasing us from stress and anxiety.

2. Drumming helps to release endorphins

Drumming can be exhilarating, exciting and help to produce the happy hormones, endorphins.

3. Drumming helps to explore all styles of music

Learning to play the drums helps us to explore all types of drums and drum styles. Whether it's carnival style Samba drumming, or sacred Native American drum circles, to playing lead drummer in a Metal, Pop, or Indie band, drums have their place in all styles of music and cultures.

4. Drumming is for all of us

Rhythm is a universal language. Everyone can enjoy the benefits of drumming and it does not matter what age, nationality, gender, or race you are.

5. Drumming boosts confidence

The main role of the drummer is to keep consistent timing for everyone else, so the responsibility can be huge but can really boost our confidence when it's done well.

6. Drumming encourages self-belief and resilience

Mastering difficult drum sections can be tricky so when it is achieved, it can inspire a great sense of self-belief and resilience.

7. Drumming improves concentration

Science shows that drumming activates the brain and stimulates it in a more complex way than people realise, which is why it has often been used in music therapy for children with ADHD to regain focus and build new neural pathways in the brain.

8. Drumming keeps us fit

Drumming uses a lot of physical energy, so it's a great cardiovascular exercise and perfect for burning calories.

9. Drumming trains your musical ear

Once you've mastered basic drum rhythms it is said that it's much easier to learn other styles of drumming from a wide variety of music.

10. Drumming encourages friendship

Playing the drums is the perfect opportunity to meet other musicians and build friendships with other people who share similar interests.

RECORD YOUR DRUMMING EXPERIENCE BELOW

What particular drumming style do you like the sound of most and why?

_____

_____

Do some research and make a list of some fun drumming opportunities in your local area then make contact:

Drum school or group name	Days and times they meet	Contact number

SUCCESS!!

If you were successful in finding your ultimate drum dream, write down your experience below.

_____

_____

_____

ART THERAPY

GET CREATIVE

Being artistically creative can help us to express any feelings that we might find difficult verbally, and you don't need to have any skills or experience to do it.

Being creative has so many health benefits from relieving stress and anxiety to feeling inspired, and it's great for boosting self-esteem.

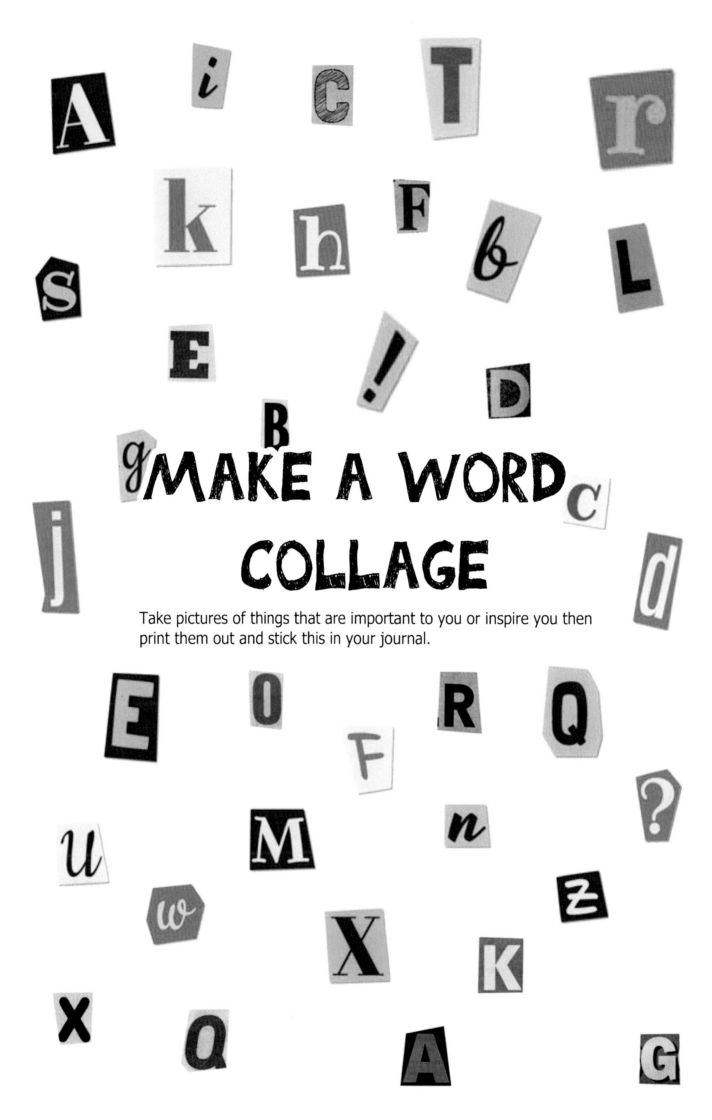

MAKE A WORD COLLAGE

Take pictures of things that are important to you or inspire you then print them out and stick this in your journal.

MAKE A PICTURE
COLLAGE

Take pictures of things that are important to you or inspire you then print them out and stick these in your journal.

MY PiCTURE COLLAGE!

WRITE A POEM OR SHORT STORY!

Get creative and write whatever comes into your mind. It can be a poem, some lyrics, or a short story. Whatever feels right, put your pen to paper and let your creativity flow.

WRITE YOUR POEM/STORY

SELF PORTRAIT

GET CREATIVE AND DRAW AN IMAGE OF YOURSELF THAT PORTRAYS ONE OR ALL OF THE QUESTIONS BELOW.

How do you see yourself now?

How do you see yourself in the future?

How do you think others see you?

DRAW YOUR PORTRAIT

Rope Swing Visualisation

Imagine in front of you stands a dense forest full of the tallest trees you have ever seen. Some are as high as skyscrapers and as tall as a house. These trees are hundreds of years old and wiser than powerful kings and queens. These trees can see every movement and speak to all other living things in the forest. These trees protect, nurture, and provide comfort to all beings that pass through.

You hear birds chattering and a soft breeze moving through the leaves as you walk in deeper and notice how thin rays of sun light beam through the trees and hit the ground in front of you, lighting up a path to a clearing within the forest. In the distance you see a long rope swing hanging from one of the tallest trees which seems like it has been placed there just for you.

You wonder how much fun it would be to sit on the swing and push yourself off to see how high you can go. As you walk towards the swing you notice how relaxed and calm you are feeling and how safe you feel in this wonderful place.

The swing is positioned in a perfect spot, with a strong rope and a flat smooth wooden base which looks really comfortable and safe to sit on. As you push off with your feet you then glide slowly through the air with a gentle motion, and it feels so relaxing moving forwards and backwards in this peaceful place. You stretch out your legs so you can go higher each time at a height that is comfortable, and you begin to think of all things you enjoy doing in your life such as happy family celebrations, fun with your friends, or simply time for yourself doing things you enjoy.

Rope Swing Visualisation

You also think of things that may mean big changes for you. Perhaps there have been some big changes at school or college which have been hard to get used to, or maybe you're worried about what the future holds and feel the pressures to achieve all the things you would like to. Perhaps there have been some changes in your personal life with family or friends which have been upsetting you.

Whatever these changes are, just imagine that each time you move back and forth on the swing, you begin to feel the changes bother you less and less. You notice that each time you move forward on the swing you feel calmer and more relaxed, and each time you move back you start to feel happy and safe. In fact, it doesn't matter what thoughts enter your head at this time because with each motion of the swing, any upsetting thoughts or worries just fall off you and onto the ground below.

You then realise that sometimes change is necessary and important to grow, develop, and become more resilient. These new thoughts are reassuring to you and help you to feel more confident about your future and how you will cope with things from now on. You remember that you can come back to this place in your mind whenever a change is bothering you, or you can practice this visualisation on a swing in a park or forest near you.

Write or draw a picture to describe the tall tress and rope swing you imagined here:

How did it feel to swing high in this beautiful forest?

_____

_____

_____

_____

What sounds did you hear, or special memories did you have of friends or family when you were on the swing?

_____

_____

_____

CHAPTER 7
GROWING RESILIENCE & BUILDING CONFIDENCE

7 ways to help your self-esteem!

7 WAYS TO HELP YOUR SELF-ESTEEM

 BE YOURSELF

 ENJOY YOUR INTERESTS

 MAINTAIN PERSPECTIVE

 MANAGE STRESS

 BE KIND TO OTHERS

 STAY HEALTHY

 BE CONFIDENT

SELF ESTEEM TABLE

Date When did the event take place?	Location Were you in a place you had been to before or somewhere new?	How did you feel? Were you nervous? Write on a scale of 1-10 (10 being the worst).	Why did you feel that way? Did someone upset you or were you hard on yourself? Or were you triggered?	What was the affect on your confidence? How has this event effected your confidence?	What have you learnt? What did you do to leave the situation or feel better? What will you do differently next time?

WHAT IS RESILIENCE?

RESILIENCE IS THE ABILITY TO COPE WHEN THINGS GO WRONG AND BEING ABLE TO BOUNCE BACK AFTER DIFFICULT TIMES. TO BE RESILIENT IS TO BE ABLE TO COPE WITH WHAT LIFE THROWS AT YOU AND SHRUG IT OFF.

How do we build resilience?

Pushing through the hard times to reach personal goals

Trying new things and taking healthy risks

Being kind and forgiving to others who make mistakes

Being mindful of others even when you feel low

Being a positive role model and speaking up for what is right

Being able to laugh at yourself and not take yourself too seriously

Not holding onto fear and anxiety and staying strong

Being true to yourself and always moving forward

REMEMBER, YOU CAN'T ALWAYS CONTROL WHAT HAPPENS TO YOU, BUT YOU CAN CONTROL HOW YOU REACT!

WHEEL OF RESILIENCE

SIMPLY THROW A DICE AND READ OUT THE SCENARIOS

You can do this challenge on your own or ask other people
you trust to do it with you so you can discuss your answers.

2 You want to join a local sports club but you are nervous of being rejected.

3 Your family pet has recently passed away.

1 A kid in school has started being mean to you and you are worried that it may get worse.

4 You didn't get into your first choice of college/course.

8 Your parents have just told you they are going to separate/divorce.

5 You failed a prep exam and the teacher is giving you extra work to keep up with your peers.

7 You've noticed someone has said something mean about you on social media.

6 Your best friend is moving across the country.

WHEEL OF RESILIENCE

CHOOSE WHAT OPTION YOU THINK IS BEST FOR THAT SITUATION

1 DO YOU

A. Do nothing and hope they get bored?

B. Confront the bully and report it to the school if it continues?

2 DO YOU

A. Be brave and go along anyway for the experience?

B. Ask a friend to go with you for moral support?

3 DO YOU

A. Hold in your tears so others don't think you're weak?

B. Acknowledge your feelings of sadness and comfort others too?

4 DO YOU

A. Accept it without question as it's out of your control?

B. Ask an adult if there is a way to appeal the decision?

5 DO YOU

A. Accept you can't do any better in this subject and give up on studying?

B. Work hard and prove to yourself that you can do it with practice?

6 DO YOU

A. Get upset and angry that they are moving and stop talking to them?

B. Keep in touch and plan to meet up again as soon as possible?

7 DO YOU

A. Do the same back and say something mean about them on your social media?

B. Remind then that cyberbullying is a crime and that you willl report them?

8 DO YOU

A. Get angry and blame your parents for ruining your life?

B. Trust their decision is for the best and reassure yourself that they still love you?

109

THE RESULTS

IF YOU AGREED WITH MAINLY A ANSWERS YOU ARE ON YOUR WAY TO BECOMING MORE RESILIENT BUT HAVE A FEW MORE LESSONS TO LEARN FIRST!

IF YOU AGREED WITH MAINLY B ANSWERS YOU ARE ALREADY A RESILIENT WARRIOR!

Don't forget: learning is wisdom and wisdom is power!

5 THINGS THAT HAVE MADE YOU FEEL RESILIENT IN YOUR LIFE

TAKE A RISK

RESiLiENCE iS SOMETHiNG THAT HAPPENS AFTER WE RECOVER FROM PROBLEMS AND CHALLENGES.

The quicker we can get back up and carry on, the stronger our resilience becomes.

The more we can learn from our mistakes and failures, the stronger we'll become and the more REMARKABLE you'll be.

ARE YOU READY TO PUSH YOURSELF AND TAKE A RISK?

YOU CAN DO IT!!

Think of something you want to achieve that means stepping out of your comfort zone; something that's a bit scary but you'll know will make you feel amazing after.

HERE ARE SOME EXAMPLES...

1. You might want to play a main part in a school play but haven't had the courage to go for it before.

2. Maybe you've always wanted to learn street dancing but didn't think you could do it.

3. You could sing a song you have written yourself in front of someone you trust.

WE BELIEVE IN YOU!

GIVE YOURSELF A RESILIENCE BOOST

Push yourself out of your comfort zone and write about your experiences.

What risk did you take?

_____

_____

_____

How did you feel during the risk?

_____

_____

_____

How did you feel after?

_____

_____

_____

What encouragement would you give to someone else who was stepping out of their comfort zone?

_____

_____

_____

Lighthouse Visualisation

Image you're navigating a small fishing boat alone out at sea and a storm is quickly rolling in.

You can't get back to the shore because the sail on your boat has broken in the wind and you are drifting further out to sea. The waves are getting bigger and bigger, and the rain is coming down fast. You can see lightning hit the water with every crack of thunder, and it lights up the entire ocean, showing the size of the huge waves which are crashing and smashing against your boat.

You're worried that the boat will tip over and sink with you in it, then suddenly in the distance you see a beautiful white lighthouse appear between the waves.

It looks close enough to get to, so you paddle with all your strength and finally, you get to the lighthouse and manage to tie your boat to the edge and climb out. You notice a large wooden door on the lighthouse edge, so you try to open it and to your relief, it opens with ease and you walk inside.

It's warm and dry inside and there is a roaring wood fire and a table full of warm tasty treats like sausage rolls, jacket potatoes, warm crusty bread rolls, cheese, fruit, and hot chocolate with whipped cream and marshmallows. It's as though this spread of food and a warm room has been prepared just for you.

lighthouse Visualisation

You're exhausted but feel so proud that you managed to navigate yourself to the light house alone, in a storm and with a broken sail.
As you sit in front of the fire wrapped in a thick woollen blanket sipping hot chocolate you notice the storm calming down outside. The clouds part and the sun's rays shine down across the gentle crystal waters.
As the waves slowly rise and fall, you notice your breathing follows the same pattern, breathing in as the waves move up and out as they gently fall down, and you feel really relaxed and happy inside.

You realise that storms can be a powerful force and quite scary at times, but they always blow over eventually.
And even though it can leave you feeling a little shaken, the experience can be a valuable life lesson and really help to build resilience which will help you overcome other challenges more easily in the future.

As you fill your belly with the tasty treats and wait to be rescued, you realise what an amazing story you'll have to tell everyone.

What a brave, resilient adventurer you are!

Use the space below to draw or describe your fishing boat:

How did you feel when you were stuck out at sea in the storm?

_____

_____

_____

How did you feel when you saw the lighthouse and went inside?

_____

_____

_____

Can you think of another time where you felt challenged and developed greater resilience as a result?

_____

_____

_____

CHAPTER 8

Setting Future Goals

Write a letter to your future self

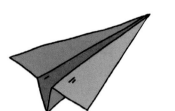
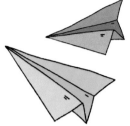

Writing a letter to your future self can be a brilliant way to see how far you've come and how many changes you've been through.
It's also a good way to check if you've reached any of the goals you set out for yourself.

IMPORTANT THINGS TO REMEMBER WHEN WRITING YOUR LETTER:

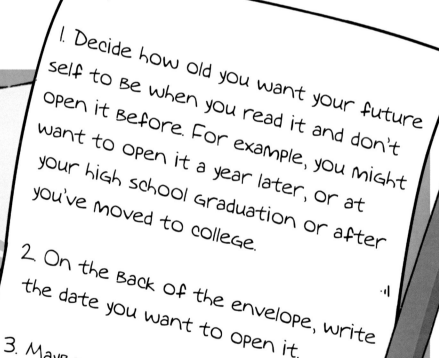

1. Decide how old you want your future self to be when you read it and don't open it before. For example, you might want to open it a year later, or at your high school graduation or after you've moved to college.

2. On the back of the envelope, write the date you want to open it.

3. Maybe you could put an object important to you in the letter. You'll have to make sure you don't lose the letter!

IF YOU NEED HELP WITH SOME IDEAS FOR YOUR LETTER, HERE'S A FEW BELOW:

- **BUCKET LIST IDEAS**

- **PLACES TO TRAVEL**

- **HOBBIES AND CLUBS**

- **SKILLS TO WORK ON**

- **BUILDING YOUR CONFIDENCE**

- **WAYS TO KEEP CALM**

- **NEW FRIENDSHIP GROUPS**

- **THINGS TO SAVE UP FOR!**

Write it as though you are writing to your best friend. Give yourself words of encouragement, tips on how to deal with stress and remind yourself how far you have come.

DEAR FUTURE ME...

MY GOALS

CREATE A VISION BOARD

MAKE A VISION BOARD WITH EVERYTHING YOU WOULD LIKE TO ACHEIVE IN THE FUTURE!

Why?

Vision boards are great because they provide you with a daily visual reminder of your dreams and goals.

Visualisation is one of the most powerful inspirations and mind workouts around.

How?

Using **A3** or **A4 plain card**, create a vision board using **pictures from magazines, newspaper, or drawings** you have created yourself.

You can decorate your vision board in any way you like. You might even want to place your board in a frame, like a piece of inspirational art!

NOW

Proudly hang or stick it in a place where you can easily see it every day as a reminder of your remarkable dreams and goals.

YOU COULD iNCLUDE:

- A house you would love to live in

- A job that you really want

- A future pet

- An event you want to go to, like a concert

- A new skill you want to learn

- A hobby you want to start/restart

Do good and good will come to you.

FRIENDS

Vision Board

CONFIDENCE
BREEDS
STRENGTH

Family

Mind Mapping

MIND MAPPING CAN HELP STRUCTURE OUR CHAOTIC THOUGHTS AND CONFUSION INTO A CLEAR PICTURE, WHICH FOR MANY PEOPLE IS MUCH EASIER TO REMEMBER THAN WORDS AND SENTENCES. IN FACT, YOU CAN USE MIND MAPPING TO HELP FOCUS, PLAN OR REMEMBER ALMOST ANYTHING.

Example:

1. Remembering new routines and activities when moving to a new school.

2. Preparing and remembering important information for essays and tests.

3. Planning and preparing a party or special event.

4. Planning and setting future goals.

Check out this example one for moving to college then do your own one for whatever subject you like on the next page:

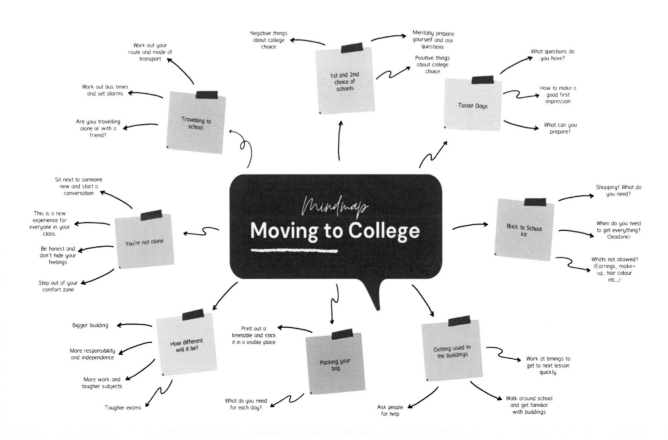

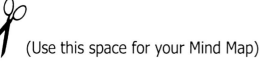 (Use this space for your Mind Map)

What does SUCCESS feel like to YOU?

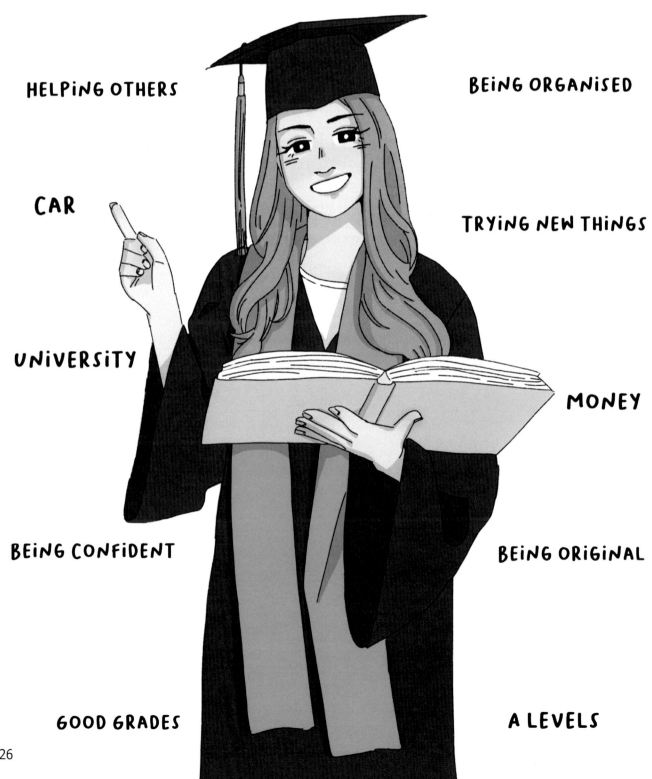

GREAT JOB

UNIVERSITY

HAVING YOUR OWN PLACE

FEELING INDEPENDENT

FEELING LOVED

HELPING OTHERS

BEING ORGANISED

CAR

TRYING NEW THINGS

UNIVERSITY

MONEY

BEING CONFIDENT

BEING ORIGINAL

GOOD GRADES

A LEVELS

What does SUCCESS feel like to YOU?

Being:

_____

_____

Feeling:

_____

_____

Knowing:

_____

_____

Starting:

_____

_____

Having:

_____

_____

The Grand Hall

Visualisation

Imagine that you are standing in front of a steep hill, thick with fresh green grass that is blowing in the wind, and at the top of the hill proudly sits a grand castle with a flag hoisted at the very top, a moat surrounding the castle and a large drawbridge at the entrance.

You walk up the hill towards the castle and as you reach the top of the hill you begin to hear voices, music, and laughter from inside, so you decide to knock on the large wooden entrance door and notice how it gently opens as you lean against it.

You decide to walk inside and are immediately greeted by a kind girl with beautiful green eyes and long red hair. She takes your hand and says, "Come, everyone is waiting for you in the Great Hall." On hearing this you start to feel really excited to learn that there is a group of people all eagerly waiting to meet you and you can't wait to see who they are.

You follow the girl along grand passageways with red carpets and walls filled with large paintings of kings and queens set in golden frames, and eventually you come to a large door with a huge brass handle.

The girl turns to you, smiles then opens the door and behind the door is stood a group of happy, smiling faces all eagerly waiting for you. Although you don't know these people or recognise their faces, you instantly feel safe and comfortable in their company, and you quickly learn that they too are in an unfamiliar place with other people they also do not know.

You were the last person who was invited to the Great Hall for a secret celebration and as you look around the room you start to feel really excited about what will happen next.

What is everyone doing here?

Why have you all been invited to this place?

What is in store for you all?

The Grand Hall

Visualisation

Suddenly you hear a bell ring, and you are all handed a warrior sword before being ushered into a long line and told that it is now time for the

'Great Intention Ceremony'

This ceremony will help to create a successful path for your future and bring much happiness as a result.

You are all asked to take a moment to think of all the positive things you want to achieve in your future then pick up your swords and point them to the sky to seal the promise and commit to those positive changes and goals in your life.

As you stand strong, with your sword held high, you realise how empowered you feel because you know that these goals you have set yourself are achievable as long as you commit to them. It doesn't matter how long they take because you know they will happen when the time is right for you and you will be supported all the way by friends and family who care about you.

You feel powerful and strong in this moment and you know that you can come back to this place in your mind whenever you want to make important decisions or even feel more confident about the decisions you have already made.

After a while, the ceremony ends, and you are satisfied with the outcome, so you decide to leave the castle and go back down the hill that led you to this amazing castle on the hill.

Your future starts here, so make it count and always look forward rather than back.

What does your castle look like? Draw or describe it here:

What does your sword look like? Draw or describe it here:

What goals and intentions did you commit to?

How did you feel when the cermony ended?

CONGRATULATIONS

- You have built up some great resilience so you can pick yourself up in challenging times.

- You have learnt how to grow your confidence and that you are willing to try new things.

- You are teaching yourself how to stay calm and more grounded, which will be an inspiration to those around you.

- And finally, your natural ability to shine brightly will attract the right kind of people to you.

WHETHER YOUR JOURNAL IS STILL A WORK IN PROGRESS, OR IF YOU HAVE COMPLETED EVERY PART, YOU ARE ON A REMARKABLE JOURNEY AND WE ARE SO GRATEFUL TO HAVE BEEN A PART OF IT!

Thank you!

Rachel Streeter

DIRECTOR OF REMARKABLE ME AND AUTHOR OF THE WELLBEING GROWTH JOURNAL

I'm Rachel Streeter, the Director of Remarkable Me and Author of the Wellbeing growth Journal for children. My therapeutic career began in London as a Mental Health Worker, then I went on to achieve two Diplomas qualifying as a Therapeutic Counsellor in 2007 and a Clinical Hypnotherapist in 2008 before setting up my private practice.

Since then I have created two therapeutic companies and developed multiple wellbeing projects and services in the community for children, families, schools and colleges.

I have since written and published the first Wellbeing Growth Journal so children can expand their creativity, develop confidence and resilience and access essential wellbeing tools each day.

I am now excited to launch the 2nd Well-being Journal for 11 - 17 year olds, so we can continue to support larger numbers of children and young people across the globe..

Gabriella Baker

SOCIAL MEDIA EXECUTIVE

Hi I'm Gabriella and I'm a social media fanatic and mum to a sausage dog called Binky.

I have always had a huge interest in mental health and well-being and have channelled this through my love of dance. At the age of 21 I graduated from Chichester University achieving a BA Hons in Dance, with a great interest in the DanceMovement Psychotherapy module. This module focused on the relational process in which a client and therapist engage in an empathetic creative process usingbody movement and dance to assist the integration of emotional, cognitive, physical, social and spiritual aspects of self.

Since graduating university I have developed a keen interest both personally and professionally in how the power of social media can influence followers. This has led to my exciting journey ahead with Remarkable Me as their Social Media Executive.

I'm excited to share all things positive and new across all our social media platforms and now with you, as you work through this wellbeing journal.

Kylla Francis

DESIGNER & DIGITAL ILLUSTRATOR

Hiya, I'm the Illustrator and digital designer on the team. Since I was young I knew I wanted to pursue a career in art. I started drawing for fun as a child but when I hit college, I knew it was something I wanted to take seriously and build as a profession.

I graduated from the University of Portsmouth in 2020 at 23 years old with a BA Hons in Illustration. My main skills are in character design and portrait illustrations, both using traditional and digital media.

I'm a huge advocate for mental health, especially for young teens, as I understand the difficulties with accepting our bodies and developing minds, so being part of this team and working on these journals is a project I'm extremely passionate about.

I'm super happy to be able to finally let you work through this book. I hope this journal can help support our readers.

Support Numbers and Websites!

(For young people)

It's always important to talk about any worries or anxieties with an adult you trust before they get any bigger and harder to deal with.

It could be a family member or a teacher ot someone else you feel safe with. It's also good to know that you can get advice and support from charities that specialise in helping children who are upset, anxious or scared.

MENTAL HEALTH SUPPORT

**www.youngminds.org.uk
85258 (YM crisis text line)**

This is a great website that offers support and advice to teens on a variety of issues and offers a crisis text line for when you need extra support.

LGBTQ+ SUPPORT

**www.youngstonewall.org.uk
0800 050 2020**

This is a brilliant website that offers specific support for LGBT/questioning teens for help with understanding and accepting who they are.

EMERGENCY

If you have an emergency or feel unsafe, you can get immediate help by calling **999** free from any phone.

Support Numbers and Websites!

(For Adults)

Supporting a child with anxiety or depression can be very worrying for parents and other family members.

Teenagers are going through a lot of changes that they might not necessary understand; but they can be resilient and work through these new challenges; but will need extra love and support.

However, if things persist it is important to seek other professional guidance, so you know how to best support your child and feel supported yourself.

There are places you can turn to for help supporting yourself and your child.

MIND.ORG.UK

email: info@mind.org.uk
phone: 0300 123 3393

Providing online advice and support to anyone experiencing any mental health problems.

SANE.ORG.UK

email: support@sane.org.uk
phone: 07984 967 708

Providing a telephone helpline or email support for anyone coping with mental illness, including concerned relatives or friends.

KIDSCAPE.ORG.UK

Providing online advice and guidance to parents and schools about bullying and how to tackle it.

SUPPORT FOR SCHOOLS + COLLEGES

We are thrilled to now offer these Wellbeing Journals to schools as part of their well-being programmes.

Schools are a vital environment for nurturing children's wellbeing and resilience; therefore it is important to identify any early behavioural changes and signs of mental distress.

There is also clear evidence that emotional wellbeing is a key indicator of academic achievement and subsequent improved outcomes later in life.

Remarkable Me practitioners and trainers have been delivering wellbeing programmes in schools and working closely with families for over 10 years.

We have always said that early intervention is key to tackling poor mental health in children and supporting a quick recovery.

Children spend most of their hours in the classroom during the day, so it is imperative that schools are in a position to fully support each child's well-being and be a key player as a....

MENTALLY HEALTHY SCHOOL

THESE JOURNALS WILL COMFORTABLY SUPPORT EACH CHILD FROM KEY STAGE 2.

BULK BUY

WE CAN PROVIDE LARGE QUANTITIES OF THESE JOURNALS STRAIGHT TO SCHOOLS AND COLLEGES AT A DISCOUNTED RATE.
PLEASE GO TO OUR WEBSITE FOR FURTHER INFORMATION.

WWW.REMARKABLEME.UK

Certificate Of Completion

Proudly presented to:

- -

for completing their wellbeing journey with honours. Well done from the Remarkable Me Team!

Rachel Streeter
Director/Author

Kylla Francis
Illustrator/Designer

Gabriella Baker
Media Executive